THE DODGERS FAN'S
LITTLE BOOK OF WISDOM

Other "Little Books of Wisdom" Titles Available

THE DODGERS FAN'S
LITTLE BOOK OF WISDOM

Kathleen McKernan

Taylor Trade Publishing
Lanham • *New York* • *Dallas* • *Boulder* • *Toronto* • *Oxford*

THE DODGERS FAN'S LITTLE BOOK OF WISDOM

Copyright © 2005 by Kathleen McKernan
First Taylor Trade Publishing edition 2005

This Taylor Trade Publishing paperback edition of *The Dodgers Fan's Little Book of Wisdom* is an original publication. It is published by arrangement with the author.

Published by Taylor Trade Publishing
An imprint of The Rowman & Littlefield Publishing Group, Inc.
4501 Forbes Boulevard, Suite 200
Lanham, Maryland 20706

Distributed by NATIONAL BOOK NETWORK

Library of Congress Cataloging-in-Publication Data
McKernan, Kathleen, 1967–
The Dodgers fan's little book of wisdom / Kathleen McKernan.—1st Taylor Trade Pub. ed.
p. cm.
Includes bibliographical references.
ISBN 1-58979-257-2 (pbk. : alk. paper)
1. Los Angeles Dodgers (Baseball team)—Miscellanea. I. Title.
GV875.L6M35 2005
796.357'64'0979494—dc22
2005004679

∞™ The paper used in this publication meets the minimum requirements of American National Standard for Information Sciences—Permanence of Paper for Printed Library Materials, ANSI/NISO Z39.48–1992.
Manufactured in the United States of America.

• Introduction •

Dodger fans are a misunderstood lot. When I was growing up in New England, the national TV cameras would show the mass exodus of the crowd to the parking lot in, oh, about the seventh inning. The message: They're not true fans.

But that's just wrong, I realized as I moved closer and then even closer to Chavez Ravine.

Sure, some fans come late and head out early—and if you've ever been caught in game-day freeway traffic around the stadium, you understand the temptation. Thousands of others stay until the end and thousands more stay glued to the radio, not even making it to the stadium. Sure, some in glamorous Los Angeles come to the park to be seen; but the Dodgers are very much a working person's team as well. The Dodger caps and car stickers are almost as ubiquitous as the Virgin of Guadalupe all over LA.

I didn't start out a Dodgers fan. Of course, I rooted for them in the World Series in the late 1970s, but I was really pulling for Anyone But the Yankees with the fervor of a preadolescent Red Sox fan.

But when my father took a job as president and general manager of the team's top minor-league affiliate, the Albuquerque Dukes, in 1979, my conversion began. I was a definite Dukes fan, and since the Dukes eventually turned into Dodgers, I was destined to be a Dodgers fan.

The Dodgers always seemed so perfect even before I became a fan. Baseball disasters didn't happen to them. Of course, there was the whole Bobby Thomson fiasco, but that was ancient history. Brooklyn Dodgers history. Even the '60s were distant for me. After all, Sandy Koufax had retired before I was born. The team itself played seemingly effortlessly, won the big games and their uniforms always seemed blindingly white and clean. And even when they lost, they didn't seem to do it quite as spectacularly as other teams. They kept their dignity.

The Dodgers who were my Boys of Summer were those of the '80s. They had their affable manager in Tommy Lasorda, who had just the right mix of intensity and bleeding-Dodger-blue schtick. Once I had been brought into the fold, though, the losses got considerably more painful, made worse by the fact that the players now on the field were oftentimes former members of my beloved Dukes. The losses, involving late-inning home runs, also became more spectacular.

We won't even talk about the horrors of some of the teams of the '90s.

Even so, Dodgers fans aren't like Red Sox fans or Cubs fans, some of whom almost seem to revel in That Which Is Pathetic. Dodgers fans expect winners. And there's been some hard times over the past 15 years. The team that seemed to epitomize stability, loyalty, class and winning baseball got sold—twice!—and went through many field and front-office changes.

And we Dodgers fans don't like it.

In a constantly changing city, the Dodgers have represented stability. It's no wonder we holler when the trades come fast and furious as has happened in recent years. We don't want the Dodgers to be as chaotic as the rest of Los Angeles, which values newness and youth and change. Dodger Stadium offers a calming piece of greenness and take-your-breath-away beauty, even while cars sit and honk on clogged freeways all around it. It seems ludicrous to imagine if you don't live in LA, but the Dodgers, in town for not quite 50 years, are a longtime tradition.

This book celebrates the winning aspect of that tradition, relishes the successful season and does its best to avoid wallowing in woe, although some of that is impossible to avoid. There *is* wisdom to be gained in baseball tragedies. Dodger fans have suffered their share of frustration in recent years, and there's no point in playing ostrich about it. Why, oh why, for example, did Tom Niedenfuer pitch to Jack Clark? (See No. 73) And the entire 1992 season is well worth forgetting (See No 52), if only we could.

Along with the lamentations, there's the humorous, the ironic and the purely inspirational bits of Dodger history that are worth reliving, or hearing about for the first time. I hope the longtime as well as newer Dodger fans will find some nuggets of interest in this work. And I hope to see you at the ballpark—still in your seat in the ninth inning!

—Kathleen McKernan
Culver City, 2004

Be True to Your Word

Sandy Koufax signed with the Dodgers for $20,000, including a $14,000 bonus, after making a verbal agreement. After the handshake deal, the Pirates offered $25,000 and the Braves $30,000. But Koufax had given his word. He became a Dodger in 1954.

Know Thyself. . .

"If someone came up to me and said he's with the Padres, I would say 'When did you become a priest?' If someone came up to me and said he was with the Indians, I'd ask what reservation he came from; if he said he was a Twin, I'd ask, 'Where's your brother?' If he said he was a Cardinal, I'd pat him on the back and say, 'Work hard, the next step is to be pope. But if someone comes up to you and says he's a Dodger, you know he's in major league baseball."

—Dodger manager Tommy Lasorda

. . . Even If You Keep Changing Your Name

The team that is now the Los Angeles Dodgers used to be known as the Trolley Dodgers, the Superbas, the Bridegrooms and the Robins, the last after manager Wilbert Robinson. Robinson led the team for 18 years starting in 1914.

"Keep Your Eye on the Ball and Hit 'Em Where They Ain't."

—Hall-of-Famer and former short-time Brooklyn Superba "Wee Willie" Keeler, on the not-so-fine points of hitting.

Every Win Counts

In the strike-shortened 1981 season, Fernando Valenzuela's 13-7 record earned him the Rookie of the Year and the Cy Young Award, the only player ever to win both in the same year.

There's Power in Positive Thinking . . .

"You must never even think, 'I can't hit this guy.' What you've got to be saying is, 'This guy can't get me out.' You have to really believe you are the best hitter in baseball."

—Lasorda, talking to Wes Parker and undoubtedly many other Dodger hitters over his coaching career. After Lasorda's pep talk during spring training of 1970, Parker went on to hit .319 and drive in 111 runs.

. . . But Only So Much Power

Lasorda's own playing career with the Dodgers ended in 1956 when he was sent down to Montreal to make room on the roster for another lefty pitcher—Sandy Koufax. He had pitched 13 innings with the Dodgers and had an ERA of 7.62. He left his legacy not as a player, but as team manager from 1976 to 1996.

Nothing's Impossible

Kirk Gibson didn't dress for Game 1 of the 1988 World Series. He could barely walk because of injuries to both legs. So it looked hopeless when he limped up to the plate as a pinch hitter in the bottom of the ninth inning against A's ace reliever Dennis Eckersley. Then it happened. With two outs and a count of 3-and-2, Gibson slammed Eckersley's slider into the right-field stands to give the Dodgers a stunning 5-4 win. Broadcaster Vin Scully commented, "In a year that has been so improbable, the impossible has happened."

Believe

And broadcaster Jack Buck summed up Gibson's home run like this:
"I can't believe what I just saw."

Don't Put a Cork in It!

Rookie second baseman Wilton Guerrero shattered his bat when he led off on June 1, 1997. After the umpires discovered the bat was "enhanced" with cork, he was ejected, fined and suspended for eight games.

There's No Place Like Home

The Dodgers broke the 3-million mark for attendance during their pennant-winning 1977 season. It was the first time any team had drawn that many fans.

Embrace Diversity

The Dodgers not only had Jackie Robinson, the first African-American baseball player in the major leagues, but their roster has boasted stars from all over the world. Fernando Valenzuela came from Mexico. Pedro Guerrero and Odalis Perez hailed from the Dominican Republic. The Dodgers signed the first Japanese-born player in Hideo Nomo. Chan Ho Park and Hee Seop Choi are both from South Korea. Craig Shipley was born in Australia. And Eric Gagne is a French Canadian.

Find Allies in Obvious (and Not-So-Obvious) Places

When Jackie Robinson made the team, he formed a double-play combination with Kentuckian Pee Wee Reese. Although some of the Southern-born ballplayers scorned Robinson's addition to the team, Reese literally would embrace him right in the middle of the field.

And a Child Shall Lead Them

Twenty-three-year-old Johnny Podres was a surprise World Series hero in 1955 when his pitching beat the Yankees 8-3 in Game Three and 2-0 in Game Seven. It was the Dodgers only World Championship in Brooklyn.

You *Can* Go Home Again

Steve Garvey was the batboy for the Dodgers during spring training as a teen in the 1960s. In the 1970s, he became the Dodgers starting first baseman.

Keep the Game in Perspective

When asked why he was quitting pitching at the top of his game after the 1966 season, Sandy Koufax said, "When I'm 40 years old, I'd still like to be able to comb my hair."

Teammates (Eventually) Do Better When They Stick Together

Sandy Koufax and Don Drysdale wanted better contracts before the 1966 season. So they held out for them together. It was the first time in history that players had staged a joint holdout. They didn't get the $500,000 each they wanted, however. Koufax got $130,000 and Drysdale got $105,000.

18

Sometimes Big Risks
Pay Big Gains

After the 1974 season, Dodgers pitcher Tommy John underwent experimental ligament surgery and it was considered unlikely that he would ever pitch again. Dr. Frank Jobe's operation, however, allowed John to come back in 1976 at better than full strength. He had his three 20-game-winning seasons after the surgery. The surgery is now named for John rather than Jobe.

Wet Fields Will Slow You Down

In 1962, Maury Wills was on his way to setting a then-major-league record with 104 stolen bases. To stop him, since nothing else would, the dreaded Giants resorted to wetting down the infield. The Dodgers protested this action, but it got San Francisco manager Alvin Dark the nickname, "The Swamp Fox."

20

Don't Take Anything *Personally*

Dodger General Manager Paul de Podesta set off a firestorm of fan reaction when he traded popular catcher Paul Lo Duca and other popular players just before the Aug. 1 interleague trading deadline in 2004 with the team in first place. "It's just business," he said.

Don't Take *Anything* Personally

In one of former Dodger General Manager Al Campanis's first trades
as GM, he traded his son, Jim, to Kansas City.

Stick with a Winning Combination

The Dodgers kept the same starting infield of Steve Garvey, Davey Lopes, Bill Russell, and Ron Cey from 1974 to 1981.

Capture the Flag

On April 25, 1976, two fans ran out onto the field at Dodger Stadium and attempted to set a U.S. flag on fire behind second base. Future Dodger player and broadcaster Rick Monday was playing center field for the Cubs that day. The flag was doused with lighter fluid, but Monday snatched it before it could go up in flames.

24

Salute Fallen Heroes

An exhibition game played on May 7, 1959, in tribute to Dodgers
catcher Roy Campanella, who had been paralyzed in an auto accident
in January 1958, drew 93,103 fans to Memorial Coliseum, the largest
crowd ever to attend a major-league game.

Shoot for the Moon

Wally Moon became known for his moonshots over the short porch at Memorial Coliseum, where the Dodgers played from 1958 to 1961. The 42-foot-screen aimed to make the stadium, which was designed for football and had a left field line of only 251 feet, a little less terrifying for Dodger pitchers.

26

Don't Talk Stupid

Longtime General Manager Al Campanis lost his job when he said on the television show *Nightline* that blacks lacked "the necessities" to be in baseball management. Campanis, who had been a minor-league teammate and roommate of Jackie Robinson's, later argued that he was talking about experience and background, not inherent abilities.

Friends Stick Together

Players of all races defended Campanis. Former Dodger outfielder
Dusty Baker said: "You hate that any man's career is ruined in a couple
of minutes. What he said was wrong, but he was always cool to
minorities when I was there, especially the Latin players and the
blacks."

Loyalty Pays Off

In 23 years as Dodger manager, Walter Alston led the team to four World Championships, including one in Brooklyn and three in Los Angeles. His successor, Tommy Lasorda, had an equally impressive record. No one can match Vin Scully, though, who has been the voice of the Dodgers for more than 50 years.

Starting out Well Is Half the Battle

Rookie pitcher Fernando Valenzuela shut out Houston, 2-0, on Opening Day in 1981. Including some appearances at the end of 1980, Valenzuela kicked off his major-league career with 34⅓ innings without giving up a run. Fernando-mania begins!

Keep Your Bat to Yourself

Juan Marichal of the dreaded Giants took a bat to the head of
Dodgers catcher John Roseboro during a brawl in 1965.

31

Keep Your Bat to Yourself, Part II

Pedro Guerrero didn't learn anything from that incident, as he threw his bat at David Cone after being hit by a pitch in a Dodgers loss to the Mets in 1988 and was suspended for four games.

Real Teams Don't Need Mascots

Manager Tommy Lasorda hated the team mascots that were all the rage in the 1980s and beyond. On Aug. 29, 1989, the Expos mascot, Youppi, was ejected from the game for annoying the Dodgers skipper during a game that was scoreless through 21 innings. It took a Rick Dempsey home run in the 22nd to end the game.

Assume Nothing

When told that teammate Sandy Koufax had thrown a no-hitter, Don Drysdale, well-aware of his light-hitting teammates, asked, "Did we win?"

Know Where the Foul Line Is

In 1978, Don Sutton upset Steve Garvey with some remarks to a reporter about his value to the team. The fists didn't start flying, however, until Sutton reportedly criticized Garvey's wife, Cyndy, as well.

It's a Head Game

Second baseman Steve Sax found himself suddenly unable to throw the ball accurately to first base in 1983. It would land in the stands or the dugout. He finished with 30 errors before settling down near the end of the season.

Damn Yankees!

Twice in the '70s and six times in the '40s and '50s, the Dodgers
won the National League pennant, only to fall to the Bronx Bombers
in the World Series.

"Chemistry Is All about Winning."

Infielder Alex Cora quoted in the *Los Angeles Times* in 2004, in effect defending a rookie General Manager Paul de Podesta's trade of popular catcher Paul Lo Duca. The trade had been denounced as destroying the first-place team's chemistry.

38

From Cy Young to "Sayonara" Run Support

Orel Hershiser won the Cy Young Award in 1988 with a 23-8 record and a 2.26 ERA. In 1989, despite an ERA of 2.31, he finished with a 15-15 record.

39

Don't Be too Loose

Kirk Gibson threw a fit in spring training of 1988 after a prankish teammate put eyeblack on the inside of his cap. Although he downplays the effects of the tantrum now, Gibson, according to the legend, chewed out the Dodgers for not taking things seriously enough. The team went on to win the pennant and the World Series.

In LA, Anyone Can Be a Celebrity

Roger Owens, a peanut seller at Dodger Stadium, has a website,
press kit, and a biography and has demonstrated his craft on
The Tonight Show.

Not with a Bang, but with a Whimper

Only 6,702 fans came to the final game at Ebbets Field in Brooklyn on September 24, 1957.

Fair Is Foul, and Foul Is Fair

As a player for the Brooklyn Dodgers, Casey Stengel once hit a ball that went foul and was called as such by the umpire. When it suddenly rolled fair before passing first base, Stengel was tagged by the first baseman, who had fielded the grounder. And then Stengel was called out.

43

Exuberance Is Forever

When feeling down, just remember Kirk Gibson limping around the basepaths with his fists pumping.

Neither a Borrower,
Nor a Lender Be

Dodger Stadium is one of only three privately owned ballparks in the
major leagues. The other two are Yankee Stadium and PacBell Park
in San Francisco.

Getting and Spending,
We Lay Waste Our Powers

The Dodgers have frequently been burned when they open up the
checkbook to sign high-priced free agents. Don Stanhouse,
Darryl Strawberry, and Eric Davis all fizzled once they put on the
Dodger Blue.

Some Are Born Great

Jackie Robinson, the first African-American player in the major leagues, was chosen for extraordinary athletic ability and extraordinary character. He finished with a lifetime .311 average; his uniform number is retired; and, although he died in 1972, his achievements placed him in the Baseball Hall of Fame.

Some Achieve Greatness

Catcher Mike Piazza was drafted in the 62nd round of the 1988 amateur draft more as a gesture of goodwill since he was the godson of manager Tommy Lasorda. The player no one really wanted was named the National League Rookie of the Year in 1993.

48

Some Have Greatness Thrust upon Them

In 1988, the Dodgers bench players, including Mickey Hatcher, Dave Anderson, Franklin Stubbs, Rick Dempsey, and Tracy Woodson, named themselves the "Stuntmen" because they were filling in for the stars on the field. The Stuntmen, however, came through time after time, helping the Dodgers hang on during a season when their starters were often injured.

Ask for Divine Intervention

"I pray, 'Please don't let the batter hit the ball to me,'" said Pedro Guerrero in 1983 when he was struggling at third. "And while I'm asking, don't let him hit it to Saxy either." Guerrero was referring to second baseman Steve Sax, who that year made a record 30 errors.

And Just Barely Old Enough to Run for President

Sandy Koufax at 36 becomes the youngest player elected to the Baseball Hall of Fame on January 19, 1972.

The Pen Is Mightier Than the Punch

Steve Garvey, despite not being on the punch-out All-Star game ballot in 1974, was voted starting first baseman thanks to write-in votes. He was that game's MVP, as well as the season's MVP for the National League that year.

Errors Will Do You In

In 1992, the Dodgers led the major leagues in errors, including 42 for shortstop Jose Offerman, on their way to a 99-loss season, the worst since 1908.

Nothing Is Certain but Death and Taxes

The O'Malley family, owners of the Dodgers for 47 years, sold the team for $311 million to Australian Rupert Murdoch. The reason for the sale, according to Dodgers president and co-owner Peter O'Malley, was to avoid triggering tax problems for those who would be inheriting the team—his children and his nieces and nephews.

The Times They Are A-Changin'

The Dodgers had two managers—Lasorda and Walter Alston—for
42 years. The next two managers did not last three seasons combined.

Don't Show Up the (New) Boss

General Manager Fred Claire called a press conference, disavowing any knowledge of an unpopular 1998 trade that sent catcher Mike Piazza to the Marlins. He was fired soon afterwards.

What's in a Name?

The Dodgers had two Mike Marshalls. One, a rotund relief pitcher, was famous for his Cy Young award and Ph.D. The other, a right fielder, became more known for his chronic injuries and for dating a rock star.

Sometimes There's Just Something in the Air

Fernando Valenzuela and former Dodger Dave Stewart, then with Oakland, threw no-hitters on the same day, June 29, 1990.

Don't Even Think "What If"

The Dodgers traded Pedro Martinez for Delino DeShields in 1993. DeShields, a slick-fielding second baseman, seemed ideal to strengthen the team up the middle. After three injury-plagued seasons in which he never hit higher than .256, he became a free-agent and left LA. Martinez went on to become one of the most dominating pitchers of the 1990s, winning the Cy Young Award three times.

One Good Draft Can Do Wonders

In the 1968 amateur draft, the Dodgers picked up the heart of their championship teams in the '70s. In that single year's worth of draft choices the team acquired: Davey Lopes, Bill Buckner, Steve Garvey, and Ron Cey and also other future big leaguers in Geoff Zahn, Tom Paciorek, Bobby Valentine, Joe Ferguson, and Doyle Alexander.

Don't Sweat the Small Stuff— Like Dirty Hats

Eric Gagne's dirty hat in 2004 might not have passed a white-glove test, but he cleaned up coming out of the bullpen. That year, he set a record of 84 consecutive saves, which he started working on in 2002.

61

Keep Expectations High

After he finally blew a save and was struggling a little, critics questioned what was wrong with closer Gagne. "What are you comparing it to?" manager Jim Tracy said in the *Los Angeles Times*, "Invincibility?"

Watch Each Other's Backs

Dodger president Peter O'Malley was known for buying up awards
from pawnshops that at least one down-on-his-luck former Dodger
had hocked.

Spread Out the Hitting

On 1977's pennant-winning team, four players (Ron Cey, Steve Garvey, Reggie Smith, and Dusty Baker) each hit 30 home runs, the first time in history that had ever been done.

Keep It in the Family

In 1968, Don Drysdale broke a 55-year-old record of consecutive
scoreless innings pitched with 58.2. In 1988, the record fell again, by
another Dodger, when Orel Hershiser went 59 innings without giving
up a run in the regular season.

And Keep History in Perspective

Even for historian Doris Kearns Goodwin, the "shot heard 'round the world" was forever the Bobby Thomson home run off Ralph Branca in the bottom of the ninth at the Polo Grounds playoff in 1951.

There's No Need for Repetition

One, "The Giants win the pennant!" was more than enough.

Focus on the Farm System

Longtime Dodger exec Branch Rickey is widely credited with inventing the baseball farm system. That farm system has produced 16 winners of the Rookie of the Year Award since 1947, when Jackie Robinson took the first one.

There's Courage in Silence

Branch Rickey, who is also credited with speeding the integration of baseball, sought out a player who would use his skills rather than his fists to silence opponents. He found one in Jackie Roosevelt Robinson, who put up with extreme verbal abuse and cheap shots on the field, without any retaliation except with his powerful bat.

Keep 'Em off the Plate

Don Drysdale in the '60s became infamous for his willingness to pitch inside, sometimes way inside, to keep the hitters off balance.

Leave Courtesy to Miss Manners

Pee Wee Reese once got tagged out at first in between pitches after he stepped off the bag to hand an errant bat back to Dixie Walker. It had slipped out of Walker's hands on a foul ball.

Wait and See

When the Dodgers traded $100 million veteran pitcher Kevin Brown to the Yankees before the 2004 season for 2003 World Series goat Jeff Weaver, many fans were annoyed. Weaver went on to put up better numbers than Brown, and Brown, a noted hothead, went on to break his hand in a fight with a concrete wall.

Don't Mess with a Man's Cap

When a fan in Wrigley Field snatched catcher Chad Kreuter's cap, the catcher went after him into the stands. Fifteen other Dodgers followed. The embarrassing melee earned the Dodgers hundreds of thousands of dollars in fines and suspensions.

The Middle Way
Is No Way to Pitch

Dodger relief pitcher Tom Niedenfuer was expected to intentionally or semi-intentionally walk former Giant Jack Clark, then with the Cardinals, with runners on second and third in the ninth, and with the Dodgers leading the playoff game 5-4. Instead, Niedenfuer's pitch came in over the plate, and Clark jacked it into the stands to send the Cardinals to the 1985 World Series.

Don't Get in a Hissing War with a Snake

Dodgers GM Kevin Malone got himself kicked out of San Diego's Jack Murphy Stadium in 2002 for taking on a Padres fan who was talking trash on the Dodgers.

Pick Winners in the Draft

The Dodgers of the late '80s and '90s felt the effects of losing General Manager Al Campanis, as famous as a judge of talent as he later became infamous for his racial remarks on TV. The best-performing major-league player of all the Dodgers' first-round draft picks during that period was Paul Konerko, whom the Dodgers traded.

How Are You Gonna Keep 'Em Down on the Farm?

The 1981 Albuquerque Dukes, led by future Dodger Mike Marshall, beat the parent club in a midseason exhibition game in Chavez Ravine before strike-interrupted play resumed. The team posted a 95-47 record in Triple-A competition, a winning percentage of .669.

Things Are Different in the Majors

The star individuals on the '81 Dukes team, including Mike Marshall, Greg Brock, Franklin Stubbs, Candy Maldonado, and Dave Anderson, never really enjoyed much big-league success.

If at First You Don't Succeed, Get the Surgery Again

No. 1 draft pick Darren Dreifort had the ligament surgery made famous by Tommy John not once, but twice.

Even Dodger Fans Get the Blues

And few seasons have hit more blue notes than 1973. On Aug. 30, the Dodgers were in first place, holding a four-game lead with 28 games left. The next day they lost to Houston and the following day they lost to Houston again. Then they lost three straight to the Giants and three of four to San Diego, before losing two to Cincinnati. In 12 days, they had gone from four up to five games out. It was all but over. The Reds clinched on Sept. 24.

Make the Most of Opportunity

When the Dodgers acquired veteran third-baseman Robin Ventura, they picked up one of the all-time grand slam home run hitters. Lou Gehrig is the leader with 23. Ventura hit his 18th in 2004. Ventura's feat is notable because he has so many fewer career home runs, not even 300. Gehrig had 493.

Never Give Up

The 1981 Dodgers lost their first two games to the Yankees in the World Series. They also fell behind in each of the following games before coming back to win and taking four straight to become world champions.

82

Watch Out for the Press (They Keep Score)

New Dodger owners Frank and Jamie McCourt got a not-so-warm Los Angeles welcome from skeptical fans and media in the spring of 2004. In an interview with the *Los Angeles Times*, Vice Chairman Jamie McCourt was quoted after stumbling over a question, "This is bad because you guys remember everything and you write everything down."

Look for Poetry in the Game

Vin Scully, the voice of the Dodgers for more than 50 years, snuck in his share of literary allusions, and he's legendary for painting word pictures, such as when he described the crowd during Koufax's perfect game as "29,000 people and a million butterflies."

But Know When to Keep Quiet

Scully let the crowd do the talking for him when he broadcasted Hank Aaron's 715th home run as well as when the Brooklyn team won the 1955 series.

Calling All Angels

Orange County's baseball team has no lack of Dodger connections.
Field manager Mike Scioscia and Mickey Hatcher both coached or
played in the Dodger farm system.

We'd Rather Have a Pennant

From 1992 to 1996, every National League Rookie of the Year wore
Dodger Blue. The five, in order, were Eric Karros, Mike Piazza,
Raul Mondesi, Hideo Nomo, and Todd Hollandsworth.

Some Things Defy Description

Hall of Fame relief pitcher Dennis Eckersley, comparing his stuff to closer Eric Gagne in the *Riverside Press-Enterprise*: "I never threw that hard. I never had a changeup from hell or whatever that thing is."

Revenge Is Sweet

"Is Brooklyn still in the league?" said Giants manager Bill Terry when asked what he thought the Dodgers would do in 1934, at a time when they were admittedly struggling. They ended up spoilers in the pennant race, beating Terry's team in their final two games, which gave the World Series berth to the Cardinals.

Don't Worry about the Weather

It took five years of play in Los Angeles before the first Dodger game
got rained out, on April 27, 1967.

Join the Club

Shawn Green hit four homers against the Milwaukee Brewers on May 23, 2002, and went 6-for-6 in the game. In franchise history, only Gil Hodges had hit that many home runs in one game.

Be Up for a Challenge

Hideo Nomo's September 17, 1996, no-hitter against the Rockies took place in Colorado's Coors Field, a notorious hitter's park.

Good Defense Can Keep You in the Game

Brooklyn catcher Bill Bergen was known as a defensive specialist—to the extreme—when he played for the Dodgers from 1904–1911. At 184 pounds with a lifetime batting average of .170, he was a Dodger who literally couldn't hit his weight.

93

Be Dignified

Low-key manager Walter Alston led the Dodgers to four World Series
crowns, the most of any National League manager, as he piloted the
team from 1954 to 1976. He won 2,040 games and never once had
more than a one-year contract.

Roll with the Changes

As the Brooklyn Dodgers transformed into the Los Angeles Dodgers, the change in ballpark forced a change in playing style, since Dodger Stadium favored the pitcher. Manager Walter Alston won both with the power hitters in Brooklyn and the power pitchers in L.A.

Run, Run, Run

In 1962, Maury Wills won the Most Valuable Player Award, while setting a (since broken) base-stealing record. He was caught only 13 times on his way to stealing 104 bases. The previous mark was 96 by Ty Cobb.

Stay with the Ship

After getting swept in the 1966 World Series, the Dodgers went on a tour of Japan. Maury Wills went home in the middle of it without telling manager Walter Alston. Wills was traded before the next season started.

If It's Broke, Fix It

In addition to Tommy John, past and present Dodgers including
Eric Gagne, Darren Dreifort, and Odalis Perez had the ligament
surgery made famous by team physician Frank Jobe and named after
Tommy John.

The Older the Fiddler, the Sweeter the Tune

Gold Glove winner Steve Finley joined the Dodgers in midseason 2004. Finley, who had also played on a World Championship team with the Arizona Diamondbacks, still played the physically demanding position of center field at the age of 38.

Winning Is a Habit.
Unfortunately, So Is Losing.

The Dodgers of the late '70s and '80s were in the winning habit. The
Dodgers of much of the '90s were, uh, *not*.

There's No Time Like the Present

. . . to break bad habits.

Think Blue

"Bleeding is unnecessary."

102

"It's a Mere Moment in a Man's Life between the All-Star Game and an Old Timer's Game."

—Vin Scully

About the Author

When she was a child, Kathleen McKernan attended games at dozens of minor-league ballparks on the East Coast. She was tagging along with her father, the late Pat McKernan, who was then president of the Eastern League. When he moved the family to Albuquerque, N.M., in 1980 to run the Dodgers' AAA farm club, she began to pull for the parent club—although she'd rooted for them in the World Series in the late 1970s.

Formerly a clutch reporter and copy editor for daily newspapers, she now comes off the bench as a freelance writer for newspapers and magazines. She also is managing editor for *New Beginnings*, a bimonthly magazine for English-speaking members of La Leche League International, an organization that focuses on breastfeeding research and support.

She has shared family memberships in the Society of American Baseball Research first with her father and now with her husband, Paul Whitfield, the author of *The White Sox Fan's Little Book of Wisdom*. Her senior thesis at the University of Notre Dame was on baseball literature.

She lives with her husband and their four children on the Westside of Los Angeles, where she's always ready to take them out to a ball game.

Bibliography

www.BaseballLibrary.com

www.baseball-reference.com

Delsohn, Steve. *True Blue: The Dramatic History of the Los Angeles Dodgers, Told by the Men Who Lived It.* New York: Morrow, 2001.

Honig, Donald. *The Los Angeles Dodgers: The First Quarter Century.* New York: St. Martin's Press, 1983.

Los Angeles Dodgers 2004 Media Guide. Los Angeles, 2004.

McNeil, William. *The Dodgers Encyclopedia.* Champaign, IL: Sports Publishing, 1997.

Palmer, Pete and Gary Gillette, eds. *The Baseball Encyclopedia.* New York: Barnes & Noble Books, 2004.

Simon, Tom, ed. *Deadball Stars of the National League.* Washington, DC: Brassey's Inc., 2004.